VOX

First Spanish Picture Dictionary

500 Brightly Illustrated Words to Start Speaking Spanish

McGraw·Hill

New York   Chicago   San Francisco   Lisbon   London   Madrid   Mexico City
Milan   New Delhi   San Juan   Seoul   Singapore   Sydney   Toronto

Table of contents
Contenido

The **McGraw·Hill** Companies

1 2 3 4 5 6 7 8 9 0   MPC/MPC   3 2 1 0 9 8 7 6 5 4

ISBN 0-07-143304-X

Illustrations by Sívia Pla Payà

McGraw-Hill books are available at special quantity discounts to use as premiums and sales promotions, or for use in corporate training programs. For more information, please write to the Director of Special Sales, Professional Publishing, McGraw-Hill, Two Penn Plaza, New York, NY 10121-2298. Or contact your local bookstore.

Good morning!
¡Buenos días!

toys
los juguetes

alarm clock
el despertador

curtain
la cortina

pajamas
el pijama

bed
la cama

pillow
la almohada

rug
la alfombra

blanket
la manta

slippers
las pantuflas

socks
los calcetines

sneakers
las zapatillas

to sleep
dormir

to get dressed
vestirse

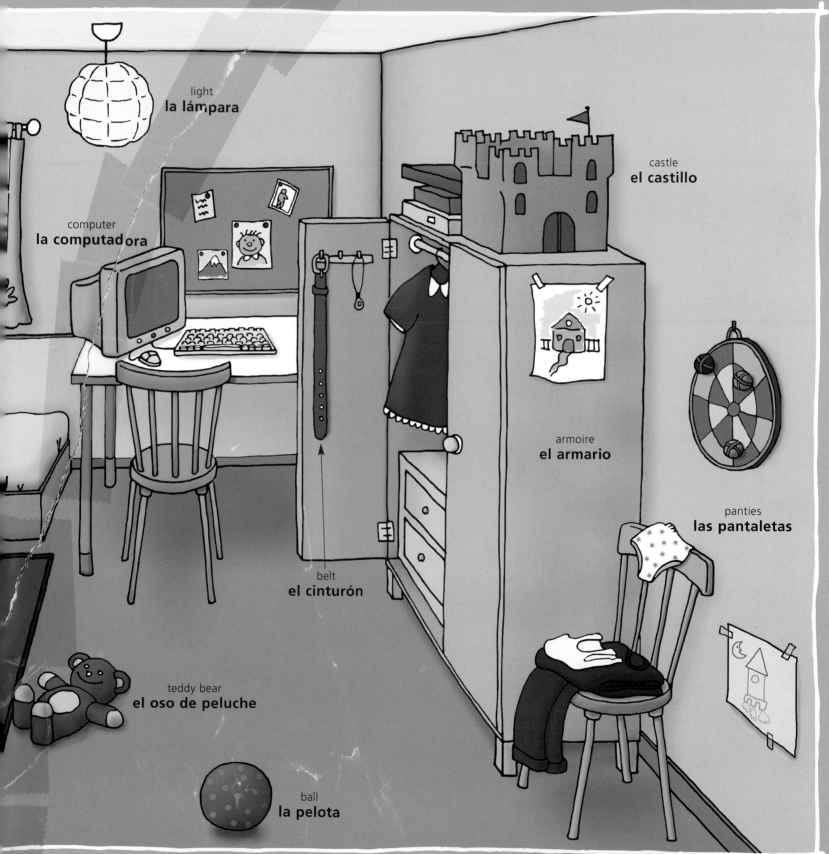

light
la lámpara

computer
la computadora

castle
el castillo

armoire
el armario

belt
el cinturón

panties
las pantaletas

teddy bear
el oso de peluche

ball
la pelota

In the bathroom
En el baño

soap
el jabón

arm
el brazo

shower
la ducha

sponge
la esponja

bathtub
la bañera

toothbrush
el cepillo de dientes

to comb
peinar

hair dryer
el secador

7

hairbrush
el cepillo

mirror
el espejo

head
la cabeza

toothpaste
la pasta de dientes

comb
el peine

toilet
el inodoro

sink
el lavabo

hand
la mano

towel
la toalla

knee
la rodilla

toilet paper
el papel higiénico

leg
la pierna

foot
el pie

Breakfast time!
¡A desayunar!

radio
el radio

cereal
los cereales

toast
la tostada

fork
el tenedor

spoon
la cuchara

milk
la leche

cup **la taza**

knife
el cuchillo

newspaper
el periódico

to hug
abrazar

orange juice
el jugo de naranja

to eat
comer

tray
la bandeja

sugar
el azúcar

yogurt
el yogur

cookies
las galletas

jam
la mermelada

butter
la mantequilla

cat
el gato

door
la puerta

En la calle

FLORISTERÍA

streetlight
la lámpara

newsstand
el quiosco

sign
**la señal
de tráfico**

magazine
la revista

bus
el autobús

blind man
el ciego

bus stop
la parada del autobús

cell phone
el celular

to read
leer

to talk
hablar

PANADERÍA

truck
el camión

car
el coche

traffic light
el semáforo

garbage can
el zafacón

scooter
la moto

police officer
la policía

mailbox
el buzón

mail carrier
el cartero

letter
la carta

12

In the classroom
En la clase

blackboard
la pizarra

calendar
el calendario

map
el mapa

chair
la silla

desk
el escritorio

eraser
el borrador

chalk
la tiza

ruler
la regla

pencil
el lápiz

pen
el bolígrafo

folder
la carpeta

sheet
la hoja

to study
estudiar

scissors
las tijeras

to write
escribir

teacher
el maestro

drawing
el dibujo

books
los libros

pencil case
el estuche

coat hook
el colgador

notebook
el cuaderno

backpack
la mochila

eraser
la goma

wastepaper basket
la papelera

The music class
La clase de música
6

score
la partitura

flute
la flauta

maracas
las maracas

chorus
el coro

guitar
la guitarra

xylophone
el xilófono

tambourine
la pandereta

drum
el tambor

piano
el piano

to sing
cantar

to hear
oír

notes
las notas

stereo
el radiocasete

trumpet
la trompeta

cymbals
los platillos

triangle
el triángulo

violin
el violín

cello
el violoncelo

conductor
la directora

In the park
En el parque
7

jungle gym
la changuera

grass
la hierba

swing
el columpio

slide
la chorrera

boy
el niño

roller skates
los patines

fountain
la fuente

bicycle
la bicicleta

friends
los amigos

to drink
beber

to run
correr

bench
el banco

see-saw
el sube-y-baja

pigeon
la paloma

girl
la niña

bucket
el cubo

jump rope
la comba

skateboard
el monopatín

sandwich
el sándwich

swan
el cisne

pond
el estanque

Happy birthday!
¡Feliz cumpleaños!

drink
el refresco

mask
la careta

candle
la vela

cake
la torta

chocolate
el chocolate

tablecloth
el mantel

doll
la muñeca

present
el regalo

candy
el caramelo

to kiss
besar

to blow
soplar

camera
la cámara de fotos

balloon
el globo

chips
las papas fritas

glass
el vaso

plate
el plato

sandwich
el sándwich

napkin
la servilleta

scooter
el patinete

Shopping
De compras

CARNICERÍA

FRUTERÍA

sausages
las salchichas

ham
el jamón

cheese
el queso

fruit
la fruta

meat
la carne

vegetables
las verduras

basket
la canasta

plant
la planta

FLORISTERÍA

flower
la flor

money
el dinero

shopping list
la lista de la compras

to buy
comprar

POLLERÍA

eggs
los huevos

chicken
el pollo

cart
el carro

mussels
los mejillónes

octopus
el pulpo

fish
el pescado

10 Clothes
La ropa

dress
el vestido

bag
la bolsa

skirt
la falda

shirt
la camisa

sweater
el jersey

jacket
la chaqueta

t-shirt
la camiseta

sales clerk
la ayudante

label
la etiqueta

shoe
el zapato

big
grande

small
pequeño

clothes
la ropa

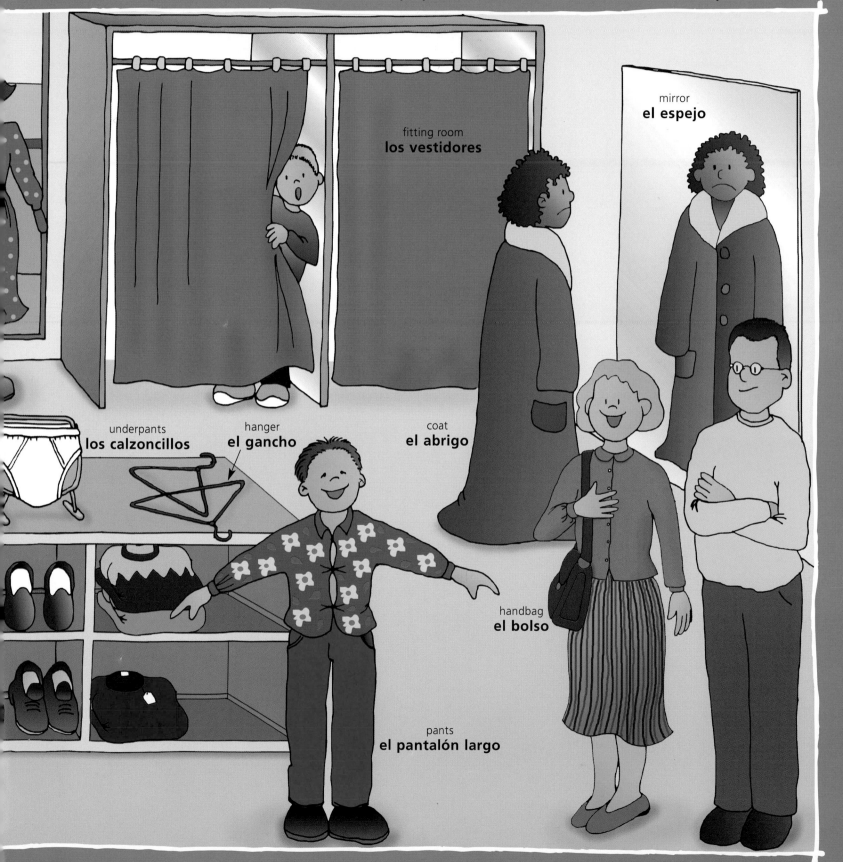

mirror
el espejo

fitting room
los vestidores

underpants
los calzoncillos

hanger
el gancho

coat
el abrigo

handbag
el bolso

pants
el pantalón largo

At the grocery store
En el supermercado

exit
la salida

entrance
la entrada

plastic bag
la bolsa

cashier
la cajera

cash register
**la caja
registradora**

shopping cart
el carro

price
el precio

credit card
la tarjeta de crédito

to take
llevar

jar
el bote

frozen food
los congelados

can
la lata

bottle
la botella

melon
el melón

pineapple
la piña

scale
la báscula

banana
la banana

potato
la papa

carrot
la zanahoria

detergent
el detergente

In the kitchen
En la cocina

clock
el reloj

range hood
la campana extractora

sponge
la esponja

cupboard
el armario

frying pan
el sartén

pot
la olla

oil
el aceite

outlet
el enchufe

stove
la estufa

microwave
el microondas

washing machine
la lavadora

to wash up
lavar los platos

food
la comida

to cook
cocinar

27

sink
el fregadero

plate
el plato

refrigerator
la nevera

telephone
el teléfono

table
la mesa

broom
el cepillo

garbage can
el zafacón

cloth
el trapo

Jobs
El trabajo

dentist
la dentista

hairdresser
el estilista

dancer
la bailarina

doctor
el doctor

nurse
la enfermera

GARAJE

cook
el cocinero

mechanic
el mecánico

waiter
el mesero

to cure
curar

to paint
pintar

to sweep
barrer

fireman
el bombero

student
la estudiante

carpenter
el carpintero

construction worker
**el trabajador
de construcción**

gardener
el jardinero

painter
el pintor

At the zoo
En el zoológico

vet
el veterinario

cub
el cachorro

elephant
el eléfante

trunk
la trompa

monkey
el chango

turtle
la tortuga

tail
la cola

ice cream
el helado

wheelchair
la silla de ruedas

butterfly
la mariposa

parrot
el loro

giraffe
la jirafa

dolphin
el delfín

tiger
el tigre

lion
el león

seal
la foca

penguin
el pingüíno

bear
el oso

15
Carnival time
En la feria

singer
la cantante

witch
la bruja

pirate
el pirata

wizard
el mago

ghost
el fantasma

robot
el robot

king
el rey

queen
la reina

cowboy
el vaquero

costumes
los disfraces

to dance
bailar

to laugh
reír

camcorder
**la cámara
de vídeo**

clown
el payaso

devil
el diablo

fairy
el hada

16
Transportation
El transporte

plane
el avión

lighthouse
el faro

bus
el autobús

car
el coche

road
la calzada

tunnel
el túnel

train
el tren

track
la vía

to drive
conducir

to fly
volar

to sail
navegar

light aircraft
la avioneta

sailboat
el velero

ship
el barco

helicopter
el helicóptero

island
la isla

boat
la barca

hot-air balloon
el globo

waterskiing
el esquí acuático

speedboat
la lancha

In the garden
En el jardín

orange
la naranja

pear
la pera

lemon
el limón

scarecrow
el espantapájaros

watermelon
la sandia

lettuce
la lechuga

cauliflower
la coliflor

pumpkin
la calabaza

to water
regar

ladybug
la mariquita

peas
los guisantes

apple
la manzana

bird
el pájaro

shovel
la pala

faucet
el grifo

horse
el caballo

bread
el pan

axe
el hacha

watering can
la regadera

tomato
el tomate

firewood
la leña

hose
la manguera

sack
el saco

In the country
En el campo
18

house
la casa

chaperone
el chaperón

boot
la bota

cap
la gorra

snail
el caracol

squirrel
la ardilla

to hike
ir de excursión

nest
el nido

mountain
la montaña

forest
el bosque

fox
el zorro

hill
la colina

flower
la flor

backpack
la mochila

stone
la piedra

water bottle
la cantimplora

pine cone
la piña

bee
la abeja

ants
las hormigas

mushroom
la seta

At the beach
En la playa

kite
la cometa

sky
el cielo

fish
el pez

wave
la ola

beach umbrella
la sombrilla

sand castle
el castillo de arena

sand
la arena

sunglasses
las gafas de sol

towel
la toalla

hot
cálido

to swim
nadar

shell
la concha

sun
el sol

windsurfing
el windsurf

lifeguard
el salvavidas

inner tube
el flotador

sea
el mar

shovel
la pala

bucket
el cubo

bathing suit
el traje de baño

bikini
el biquini

rake
el rastrillo

crab
el cangrejo

20 On the farm
En la granja

straw
la paja

field
el campo

tractor
el tractor

cow
la vaca

mouse
el raton

water
el agua

duck
el pato

farmer
el granjero

rabbit
el conejo

peacock
el pavo real

dog
el perro

sheep
la oveja

honey
la miel

to plant
plantar

cat
el gato

door
la puerta

window
la ventana

pig
el cerdo

rooster
el gallo

hen
la gallina

chicks
los pollos

21 At night
De noche

moon
la luna

star
la estrella

chimney
la chimenea

bat
el murciélago

roof
el techo

cabin
la cabaña

owl
el búho

steps
las escaleras

firewood
la leña

branch
la rama

campfire
la fogata

to yawn
bostezar

darkness
la oscuridad

to dream
soñar

tree
el árbol

light
la luz

flashlight
la linterna

rock
la roca

frog
la rana

river
el río

Christmas
La Navidad

son
el hijo

nativity
el nacimiento

stocking
el calcetín

card
la tarjeta

candy
los dulces

grandmother
la abuela

father
el padre

mother
la madre

angel
el ángel

fire
el fuego

brother   sister
el hermano   la hermana

decorations
las decoraciones

fireplace
la chimenea

Santa Claus
el Papá Noel

star
la estrella

grandfather
el abuelo

tinsel
la escarcha

daughter
la hija

Christmas tree
el árbol de Navidad

48

23
In the snow
En la nieve

cloud
la nube

glove
el guante

winter hat
la gorra

jacket
la chaqueta

ice
el hielo

skis
los esquís

snowball
la bola de nieve

scarf
la bufanda

coat
el abrigo

to ski
esquiar

to snow
nevar

cold
frío

chair lift
el teleferico

skier
el esquiador

pine tree
el abeto

snow
la nieve

snowman
el hombre de nieve

sweater
el jersey

sled
el trineo

My face
Mi cara

pigtails
las coletas

forehead
la frente

ear
la oreja

mouth
la boca

shoulder
el hombro

chin
la barbilla

fingernail
la uña

arm
el brazo

29 Numbers **Los números**

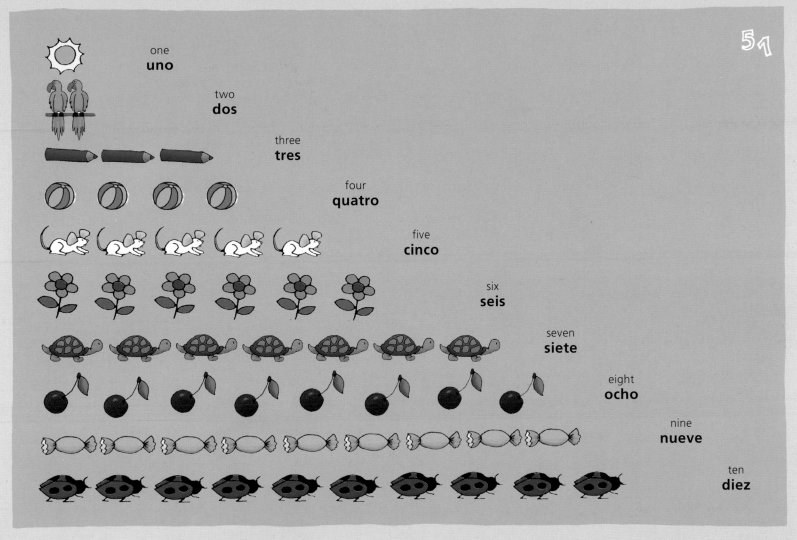

one
uno

two
dos

three
tres

four
quatro

five
cinco

six
seis

seven
siete

eight
ocho

nine
nueve

ten
diez

30 Colors **Los colores**

green
verde

yellow
amarillo

orange
naranja

red
rojo

blue
azul

white
blanco

brown
marrón

gray
gris

black
negro

pink
rosa

Indexes
Índices

Spanish-English Glossary and Pronunciation

Look at the pronunciation guide in parentheses after each Spanish word or expression in this word list. It will teach you to pronounce the Spanish words and phrases as Spanish speakers do. When you pronounce the guides out loud, read them as you would read words and syllables in English.

Here are a few hints about saying words in Spanish. The Spanish *r* is different from the English *r*. To say it correctly, "trill" the sound by flapping your tongue against the roof of your mouth once. Whenever you see *rr* in the pronunciation guide, trill the sound longer by flapping your tongue several times. The Spanish letter *ñ* is pronounced "ny." You will see it written as "ny" in the pronunciation guides. The letter *ll* is pronounced as "y" and that's how you will see it in the pronunciation. The letter *a* always sounds like the *a* in *father*. The letter *o* always sounds like the *o* in *go*. And always pronounce the letter *e* as in *let*.

Each word in the pronunciation guides has one syllable in bold letters. This is the stressed syllable. When you read the pronunciation aloud, just say the bold syllable a little louder than the others to use the correct stress. Please note that the number following the English translation refers to the unit, not the page.

A

la abeja (la a-**beh**-ha) bee 18

el abeto (el a-**beh**-toh) pine tree 23

abrazar (a-bra-**sar**) to hug 3

el abrigo (el a-**bree**-go) coat 10, 23

la abuela (la a-**bweh**-la) grandmother 22

el abuelo (el a-**bweh**-lo) grandfather 22

el aceite (el a-**say**-teh) oil 12

el agua (el **a**-gwa) water 20

la alfombra (la al-**fom**-bra) rug 1

la almohada (la al-mo-**ah**-da) pillow 1

el amarillo (el a-ma-**ree**-yo) yellow 30

los amigos (los a-**mee**-gohs) friends 7

el ángel (el **an**-hel) angel 22

el árbol (el **ar**-bol) tree 21

el árbol de Navidad (el ar-bol deh na-bee-**dahd**) Christmas tree 22

el arco iris (el **ar**-ko **ee**-rees) rainbow 26

la ardilla (la ar-**dee**-ya) squirrel 18

la arena (la a-**reh**-na) sand 19

el armario (el ar-**ma**-ree-o) armoire 1, cupboard 12

el autobús (el ow-toh-**boos**) bus 4, 16

el avión (el a-**byon**) plane 16

la avioneta (la a-byo-**neh**-ta) light aircraft 16

la ayudante (la a-yoo-**dahn**-teh) sales clerk 10

el azúcar (el a-**soo**-kar) sugar 3

el azul (el **a**-sool) blue 30

B

bailar (bigh-**lar**) to dance 14

la bailarina (la bigh-la-**ree**-na) dancer 13

el banco (el **ban**-ko) bench 7

la bandeja (la ban-**deh**-ha) tray 3

bañarse (ba-**nyar**-seh) to take a bath 2

la bañera (la ba-**nyeh**-ra) bathtub 2

el baño (el **ba**-nyo) bathroom 2

la barbilla (la bar-**bee**-ya) chin 24

la barca (la **bar**-ka) boat 16

el barco (el **bar**-ko) ship 16

barrer (ba-**rrehr**) to sweep 13

la báscula (la **bas**-koo-la) scale 11

beber (beh-**ber**) to drink 7

besar (beh-**sar**) to kiss 8

la bicicleta (la bee-see-**kleh**-ta) bicycle 7

el biquini (el bee-**kee**-nee) bikini 19

el blanco (el **blan**-ko) white 30

la boca (la **bo**-ka) mouth 24

la bola de nieve (la **bo**-la deh **nyeh**-beh) snowball 23

el bolígrafo (el bo-**lee**-gra-fo) pen 5

la bolsa (la **bol**-sa) bag 10; plastic bag 11

el bolso (el **bol**-so) handbag 10

el bombero (el bom-**beh**-ro) fireman 13

el borrador (el bo-rra-**dor**) eraser 5

el bosque (el **bos**-keh) forest 18

bostezar (bos-teh-**sar**) to yawn 21

la bota (la **bo**-ta) boot 18

el bote (el **bo**-teh) jar 11

el bote de la basura (el **bo**-teh de la ba-**soo**-ra) garbage can 4, 12

la botella (la bo-**teh**-ya) bottle 11

el brazo (el **bra**-so) arm 2, 24

la bruja (la **broo**-ha) witch 15

¡Buenos días! (**bweh**-nos **dee**-as) Good morning! 1

la bufanda (la boo-**fan**-da) scarf 23

el búho (el **boo**-oh) owl 21

el buzón (el boo-**son**) mailbox 4

C

el caballo (el ka-**ba**-yo) horse 17

la cabaña (la ka-**ba**-nyah) cabin 21

el cabello (el ka-**beh**-yo) hair 24

la cabeza (la ka-**beh**-sa) head 2

el cachorro (el ka-**cho**-rro) cub 14

el café (el ka-**feh**) brown 30

la caja registradora (la **ka**-ha reh-hees-tra-**doh**-ra) cash register 11

la cajera (la ka-**heh**-ra) cashier 11

la calabaza (la ka-la-**ba**-sa) pumpkin 17

el calcetín (el kahl-seh-**teen**) stocking 22

los calcetines (los kal-seh-**tee**-nes) socks 1

el calendario (el ka-len-**da**-ree-oh) calendar 5

calido (**ka**-lee-doh) hot 19

la calle (la **ka**-yeh) street 4

la calzada (la kal-**sa**-da) road 16

los calzoncillos (los kal-son-**see**-yos) underpants 10

la cama (la **ka**-ma) bed 1

la cámara de fotos (la **ka**-ma-ra deh **fo**-tos) camera 8

la cámara de vídeo (la **ka**-ma-ra deh **bee**-deh-o) camcorder 15

el camión (el ka-**myon**) truck 4

la camisa (la ka-**mee**-sa) shirt 10

la camiseta (la ka-mee-**seh**-ta) t-shirt 10

la campana extractora (la kam-**pa**-na ex-trak-**toh**-ra) range hood 12

el campo (el **kam**-po) country 18; field 20

la canasta (la ka-**na**-sta) basket 9

el cangrejo (el kan-**greh**-ho) crab 19

la cantante (la kan-**tan**-teh) singer 15

cantar (kan-**tar**) to sing 6

la cantimplora (la kan-teem-**plo**-ra) water bottle 18

la cara (la **ka**-ra) face 24

el caracol (el ka-ra-**kol**) snail 18

la carne (la **kar**-neh) meat 9

la carnicería (la kar-nee-seh-**ree**-a) butcher's 9

la carpeta (la kar-**peh**-ta) folder 5

el carpintero (el kar-peen-**teh**-ro) carpenter 13

el carro (el **ka**-rro) shopping cart 9, 11

la carta (la **kar**-ta) letter 4

el cartero (el kar-**teh**-ro) mail carrier 4

la casa (la **ka**-sa) house 18

el castillo (el kas-**tee**-yo) castle 1

el castillo de arena (el kas-**tee**-yo deh a-**reh**-na) sand castle 19

la catarina (la ka-ta-**ree**-na) ladybug 17

la ceja (la **seh**-ha) eyebrow 24

el celular (el seh-loo-**lar**) cell phone 4

el cepillo (el seh-**pee**-yo) hairbrush 2

el cepillo de dientes (el seh-**pee**-yo deh **dyen**-tes) toothbrush 2

el cerdo (el **ser**-doh) pig 20

los cereales (los seh-reh-**a**-les) cereal 3

la chamarra (la cha-**ma**-rra) coat 23

el chango (el **chan**-go) monkey 14

la changuera (la chan-**geh**-ra) jungle gym 7

el chaperón (el cha-peh-**rone**) chaperone 18

la chaqueta (la cha-**keh**-ta) jacket 10

la chimenea (la chee-meh-**neh**-a) chimney 21; fireplace 22

el chocolate (el cho-ko-**la**-teh) chocolate 8

el ciego (el **syeh**-go) blind man 4

el cielo (el **syeh**-lo) sky 19

cinco (**seen**-ko) five 29

el cinturón (el seen-too-**rohn**) belt 1

el cisne (el **seez**-neh) swan 7

la clase (la **kla**-seh) class 5, 6

el coche (el **ko**-cheh) car 4, 16

la cocina (la ko-**see**-na) kitchen 12

cocinar (ko-see-**nar**) to cook 12

el cocinero (el ko-see-**neh**-ro) cook 13

el codo (el **ko**-doh) elbow 24

la cola (la **ko**-la) tail 14

las coletas (la ko-**leh**-tas) pigtails 24

el colgador (el kohl-ga-**dor**) coat hook 5

la coliflor (la ko-lee-**flor**) cauliflower 17

la colina (la ko-**lee**-na) hill 18

los colores (los ko-**lo**-res) colors 30

el columpio (el ko-**loom**-pee-o) swing 7

la comba (la **kom**-ba) jump rope 7

comer (ko-**mer**) to eat 3

la cometa (la ko-**meh**-ta) kite 19

la comida (la ko-**mee**-da) food 12

comprar (kom-**prar**) to buy 9

las compras (las **kom**-pras) shopping 9

la computadora (la kom-poo-ta-**doh**-ra) computer 1

la concha (la **kon**-cha) shell 19

conducir (kon-doo-**seer**) to drive 16

el conejo (el ko-**neh**-ho) rabbit 20

los congelados (los kon-heh-**la**-dos) frozen foods 11

contento (kon-**ten**-toh) happy 24

el coro (el **ko**-ro) chorus 6

correr (ko-**rrer**) to run 7

la cortina (la kor-**tee**-na) curtain 1

el cuaderno (el kwa-**der**-no) notebook 5

cuatro (**kwa**-tro) four 29

la cubeta (la koo-**beh**-ta) bucket 7, 19

la cuchara (la koo-**cha**-ra) spoon 3

el cuchillo (el koo-**chee**-yo) knife 3

el cuello (el **kweh**-yo) neck 24

el cumpleaños (el koom-pleh-**a**-nyos) birthday 8

curar (koo-**rar**) to cure 13

D

las decoraciones (las deh-ko-ra-**syo**-nehs) decorations 22

el dedo (el **deh**-doh) finger 24

el delfín (el del-**feen**) dolphin 14

la dentista (la den-**tees**-ta) dentist 13

desayunar (des-a-yoo-**nar**) to eat breakfast 3

el despertador (el des-per-ta-**dor**) alarm clock 1

el detergente (el deh-tehr-**hen**-teh) detergent 11

los días (los **dee**-as) days 27

el dibujo (el dee-**boo**-ho) drawing 5

diez (dyes) ten 29

el dinero (el dee-**neh**-ro) money 9

la directora (la dee-rek-**tor**-a) conductor 6

los disfraces (los dees-**fra**-sehs) costumes 15

el doctor (el dohk-**tor**) doctor 13

el domingo (el doh-**meen**-go) Sunday 27

dormir (dor-**meer**) to sleep 1

dos (dohs) two 29

la ducha (la **doo**-cha) shower 2

los dulces (los **dool**-sehs) candy 8, 22

E

el elefante (el eh-leh-**fan**-teh) elephant 14

el enchufe (el en-**choo**-feh) socket 12

la enfermera (la en-fer-**meh**-ra) nurse 13

la entrada (la en-**tra**-da) entrance 11

las escaleras (las es-ka-**leh**-ras) steps 21

la escarcha (la es-**kar**-cha) tinsel 22

la escoba (la es-**ko**-ba) broom 12

escribir (es-kree-**beer**) to write 5

el escritorio (el es-kree-**toh**-ryo) desk 5

el espantapájaros (el es-pan-ta-**pa**-ha-ros) scarecrow 17

el espejo (el es-**peh**-ho) mirror 2, 10

la esponja (la es-**pohn**-ha) sponge 2, 12

el esquí acuatico (el es-**kee** a-**kwa**-tee-ko) water skiing 16

el esquiador (el es-kee-a-**dor**) skier 23

esquiar (es-kee-**ar**) to ski 23

los esquís (los es-**kees**) skis 23

las estaciones (las es-ta-**syon**-ehs) seasons 28

el estanque (el es-**tan**-keh) pond 7

el estilista (el es-tee-**lees**-ta) hairdresser 13

la estrella (la es-**treh**-ya) star 21, 22

el estuche (el es-**too**-cheh) pencil case 5

la estudiante (la es-too-dee-**ahn**-teh) student 13

estudiar (es-too-dee-**ar**) to study 5

la estufa (la es-**too**-fa) stove 12

la etiqueta (la eh-tee-**keh**-ta) label 10

F

la falda (la **fal**-da) skirt 10

el fantasma (el fan-**tas**-ma) ghost 15

el faro (el **fa**-ro) lighthouse 16

felíz (feh-**lees**) happy 8

la feria (la **feh**-rya) carnival 15

la flauta (la **flaoo**-ta) flute 6

la flor (la **flor**) flower 9, 18

el florista (el flo-**ree**-sta) florist 4, 9

el flotador (el flo-ta-**dor**) inner tube 19

la foca (la **fo**-ka) seal 14

la fogata (la fo-**ga**-ta) campfire 21

el fregadero (el freh-ga-**deh**-ro) sink 12

la frente (la **fren**-teh) forehead 24

la fresa (la **freh**-sa) strawberry 11

el frío (el **free**-o) cold 23

la fruta (la **froo**-ta) fruit 9

la frutería (la froo-teh-**rya**) fruit shop 9

el fuego (el **fweh**-go) fire 22

la fuente (la **fwen**-teh) fountain 7

G

las galletas (las ga-**yeh**-tas) cookies 2

la gallina (la ga-**yee**-na) hen 20

el gallo (el **ga**-yo) rooster 20

el gancho (el **gan**-cho) hanger 10

el garaje (el ga-**ra**-heh) garage 13

el gato (el **ga**-toh) cat 2, 20

el globo (el **glo**-bo) balloon 8; hot-air balloon 16

la goma (la **go**-ma) eraser 5

la gorra (la **go**-rra) cap 18; winter hat 23

grande (**gran**-deh) big 10

la granja (la **gran**-ha) farm 20

el granjero (el gran-**heh**-ro) farmer 20

el grifo (el **gree**-fo) faucet 17

el gris (el **grees**) gray 30

el guante (el **gwan**-teh) glove 23

los guisantes (los gee-**san**-tes) peas 17

la guitarra (la gee-**ta**-rra) guitar 6

H

hablar (a-**blar**) to speak 8

el hacha (el **a**-cha) axe 17

el hada (el **a**-da) fairy 15

el helado (el eh-**la**-doh) ice cream 14

el helicóptero (el eh-lee-**kop**-teh-ro) helicopter 16

el hermano (el er-**ma**-no) brother 22

la hermana (la er-**ma**-na) sister 22

el hielo (el **ye**-lo) ice 23

la hierba (la **yer**-ba) grass 7

la hija (la **ee**-ha) daughter 22

el hijo (el **ee**-ho) son 22

la hoja (la **o**-ha) sheet of paper 5

el hombre de nieve (el **ohm**-breh deh **nyeh**-beh) snowman 23

el hombro (el **om**-bro) shoulder 24

el hongo (el **ohn**-go) mushroom 18

la hora (la **or**-a) hour 2

las hormigas (las or-**mee**-gahs) ants 18

los huevos (los **weh**-bohs) eggs 9

I

el inodoro (el ee-no-**doh**-ro) toilet 2

el invierno (el een-**byer**-no) Winter 28

ir de excursión (eer-deh-ex-koor-see-**ohn**) to hike 18

la isla (la **ees**-la) island 16

J

el jabón (el ha-**bohn**) soap 2

el jamón (el ha-**mohn**) ham 9

el jardín (el har-**deen**) garden 13

el jardinero (el har-dee-**neh**-ro) gardener 13

la jarra (la **ha**-rra) jar 11

la jirafa (la hee-**ra**-fa) giraffe 14

el jueves (el **hweh**-bes) Thursday 27

el jugo (el **hoo**-go) juice 3

los juguetes (los hoo-**geh**-tes) toys 1

L

la lámpara (la **lam**-pa-ra) flashlight 21; light 1; streetlamp 4

la lancha (la **lan**-cha) speedboat 16

el lápiz (el **la**-pees) pencil 5

la lata (la **la**-tah) can 11

el lavabo (el la-**ba**-bo) sink 2

la lavadora (la la-ba-**dor**-a) washing machine 12

lavar los platos (la-**bar** los **pla**-tohs) to wash the dishes 12

la leche (la **leh**-che) milk 3

la lechuga (la leh-**choo**-ga) lettuce 17

leer (leh-**er**) to read 4

los lentes (los **len**-tehs) glasses 24

los lentes de sol (los **len**-tehs deh sol) sunglasses 19

la leña (la **leh**-nya) firewood 17, 21

el león (el leh-**ohn**) lion 14

los libros (los **lee**-bros) books 5

la lima (la lee-**ma**) lemon 17

la lista de compras (la **lees**-ta deh **kom**-pras) shopping list 9

llevar (yeh-**bar**) to take 11

la lluvia (la **yoo**-bee-ya) rain 26

el loro (el **lo**-ro) parrot 14

la luna (la **loo**-na) moon 21

el lunes (el **loo**-nes) Monday 27

la luz (la **loos**) light 21

M

la maceta (la ma-**seh**-ta) flowerpot 35

la madre (la **ma**-dreh) mother 22

el maestro (el ma-**es**-tro) teacher (m.) 5

el mago (el **ma**-go) wizard 15

la manguera (la man-**geh**-ra) hose 17

la mano (la **ma**-no) hand 2, 24

la manta (la **man**-ta) blanket 1

el mantel (el man-**tel**) tablecloth 8

la manzana (la man-**sa**-na) apple 17

la mañana (la ma-**nya**-na) morning 25

la mantequilla (la mahn-teh-**kee**-yah) butter 3

el mapa (el **ma**-pa) map 5

el mar (el mar) sea 19

las maracas (las ma-**ra**-kas) maracas 6

la mariposa (la ma-ree-**po**-sa) butterfly 14

el martes (el **mar**-tes) Tuesday 27

la máscara (la **mas**-ka-ra) mask 8

el mecánico (el meh-**ka**-nee-ko) mechanic 13

la mejilla (la meh-**hee**-ya) cheek 24

los mejillónes (los meh-hee-**yon**-es) mussels 9

el melón (el meh-**lon**) melon 11

el mercado (el mer-**ka**-doh) market 9

el mercado de fruta (el mer-**ka**-doh deh **froo**-ta) fruit market 9

la mermelada (la mer-meh-**la**-da) jam 3

la mesa (la **meh**-sa) table 12

el mesero (el meh-**seh**-ro) waiter 13

el microondas (el mee-kro-**ohn**-das) microwave 12

la miel (la **myel**) honey 20

el miércoles (el **myer**-ko-lehs) Wednesday 27

la mochila (la mo-**chee**-la) backpack 5, 18

el monopatín (el mo-no-pa-**teen**) skateboard 7

la montaña (la mon-**ta**-nya) mountain 18

la moto (la **mo**-toh) scooter 4

la muñeca (la moo-**nyeh**-ka) doll 8

el murciélago (el moor-**syeh**-la-go) bat 21

la música (la **moo**-see-ka) music 6

N

el nacimiento (el na-see-**myen**-toh) nativity 22

nadar (na-**dar**) to swim 19

la naranja (la na-**ran**-ha) orange (fruit) 17

el naranja (el na-**ran**-ha) orange (color) 30

la nariz (la na-**rees**) nose 24

navegar (na-beh-**gar**) to sail 16

la Navidad (la na-bee-**dahd**) Christmas 22

el negro (el **neh**-gro) black 30

nevar (neh-**var**) to snow 23

el nido (el **nee**-doh) nest 18

la nieve (la **nyeh**-beh) snow 23, 26

la niña (la **nee**-nya) girl 7

el niño (el **nee**-nyo) boy 7

la noche (la **no**-cheh) night 21, 25

las notas (las **no**-tas) notes 6

la nube (la **noo**-beh) cloud 23

nueve (**nweh**-beh) nine 29

los números (los **noo**-meh-ros) numbers 29

O

ocho (**o**-cho) eight 29

oír (o-**eer**) to hear 6

el ojo (el **o**-ho) eye 24

la ola (la **o**-la) wave 19

la olla (la **oy**-ya) pot 12

la oreja (la o-**reh**-ha) ear 24

la oscuridad (la o-skoo-ree-**dahd**) darkness 21

el oso (el **o**-so) bear 14

el oso de peluche (el **o**-so deh peh-**loo**-cheh) teddy bear 1

el otoño (el o-**toh**-nyo) Autumn 28

la oveja (la o-**beh**-ha) sheep 20

P

el padre (el **pa**-dreh) father 22

la paja (la pa-**ha**) hay 20

el pájaro (el **pa**-ha-ro) bird 17

la pala (la **pa**-la) shovel 17, 19

la paloma (la pa-**lo**-ma) pigeon 7

el pan (el pahn) bread 17

la panadería (la pa-na-deh-**ree**-a) bakery 4

la pandereta (la pan-deh-**reh**-ta) tambourine 6

las pantaletas (las pan-ta-**leh**-tas) panties 1

el pantalón (el pan-ta-**lon**) pants 10

las pantuflas (las pahn-**too**-flas) slippers 1

la papa (la **pa**-pa) potato 11

el Papá Noel (el pa-**pa no**-el) Santa Claus 22

las papas fritas (las **pa**-pas **free**-tas) potato chips 8

el papel higiénico (el **pa**-pel ee-**hyeh**-nee-ko) toilet paper 2

la papelera (la pa-peh-**leh**-ra) wastepaper basket 5

la parada de autobús (la pa-**ra**-da deh ow-toh-**boos**) bus stop 4

el parque (el **par**-keh) park 7

la partitura (la par-tee-**too**-ra) score 6

la pasta de dientes (la **pa**-sta deh **dyen**-tehs) toothpaste 2

los patines (los pa-**tee**-nehs) skates 7

el patinete (el pa-tee-**neh**-teh) scooter 8

el pato (el **pa**-toh) duck 20

el pavo real (el **pa**-bo reh-**ahl**) peacock 20

el payaso (el pa-**ya**-so) clown 15

peinar (payee-**nar**) to comb 2

el peine (el **payee**-neh) comb 2

la pelota (la peh-**lo**-ta) ball 1

pequeño (peh-**keh**-nyo) small 10

la pera (la **peh**-ra) pear 17

el periódico (el peh-**ryo**-dee-ko) newspaper 3

el perro (el **peh**-rro) dog 20

el pescado (el pes-**ka**-doh) fish 9

el pez (el pes) fish 19

el piano (el **pya**-no) piano 6

el pie (el pyeh) foot 2

la piedra (la **pyeh**-dra) stone 18

la pierna (la **pyer**-na) leg 2

el pijama (el pee-**ha**-ma) pajama 1

la piña (la **pee**-nya) pineapple 11; pine cone 18

el pingüino (el peen-**gwee**-no) penguin 14

pintar (peen-**tar**) to paint 13

la pintora (la peen-**tor**-a) painter 13

el pirata (el pee-**ra**-ta) pirate 15

el pizarrón (el pee-sa-**rron**) blackboard 5

la planta (la **plahn**-ta) plant 9

plantar (plahn-**tar**) to plant 20

el platano (el **pla**-ta-no) banana 11

los platillos (los pla-**tee**-yohs) cymbals 6

el plato (el **pla**-toh) plate 8, 12

la playa (la **pla**-ya) beach 19

la policía (la po-lee-**see**-a) police officer 4

la pollería (la poy-yeh-**ree**-a) poulterer's 9

el pollo (el **poy**-yo) chicken 9

los pollos (los **poy**-yos) chicks 20

el precio (el **preh**-syoh) price 11

la primavera (la pree-ma-**beh**-ra) Spring 28

la puerta (la **pwer**-ta) door 3, 20

el pulgar (el pool-**gar**) thumb 24

el pulpo (el **pool**-po) octopus 9

Q

el queso (el **keh**-so) cheese 9

el quiosco (el **kyo**-sko) newsstand 4

R

el radio (el **rra**-dyo) radio 3

el radiocasete (el **rra**-dyo-ka-**seh**-teh) stereo 6

la rama (la **rra**-ma) branch 21

la rana (la **rra**-na) frog 21

el rastrillo (el rras-**tree**-yo) rake 19

el ratón (el rra-**tohn**) mouse 20

el refresco (el rreh-**fres**-ko) soda 8

el refrigerador (el rreh-free-heh-ra-**dor**) refrigerator 12

la regadera (la rreh-ga-**deh**-ra) watering can 17

el regalo (el rreh-**ga**-lo) present 8

regar (rreh-**gar**) to water 17

la regla (la **rreh**-gla) ruler 5

la reina (la **rrayee**-na) queen 14

reír (rreh-**eer**) to laugh 15

el reloj (el rreh-**lo**) clock 12

la resbaladilla (la rres-ba-la-**dee**-ya) slide 7

la revista (la rreh-**bees**-ta) magazine 4

el rey (el rreh) king 15

el río (el **rree**-o) river 21

el robot (el rro-**bot**) robot 15

la roca (la **rro**-ka) rock 21

la rodilla (la rro-**dee**-ya) knee 2

el rojo (el **rro**-ho) red 30

la ropa (la **rro**-pa) clothes 10

el rosa (el **rro**-sa) pink 30

S

el sábado (el **sa**-ba-doh) Saturday 27

el saco (el **sa**-ko) sack 17

las salchichas (las sal-**chee**-chas) sausages 9

la salida (la sa-**lee**-da) exit 11

el salvavidas (el sal-ba-**bee**-das) lifeguard 19

la sandía (la san-**dee**-a) watermelon 17

el sándwich (el **san**-weesh) sandwich 7, 8

el sartén (el sar-**ten**) frying pan 12

el secador (el seh-ka-**dor**) hairdryer 2

seis (sehs) six 29

el semáforo (el seh-**ma**-fo-ro) traffic light 4

la semana (la seh-**ma**-na) week 27

la señal de tráfico (la seh-**nyal** deh **tra**-fee-ko) traffic sign 4

la servilleta (la ser-bee-**yeh**-ta) napkin 8

siete (**syeh**-teh) seven 29

la silla (la **see**-ya) chair 5

la silla de ruedas (la **see**-ya deh **rrweh**-das) wheelchair 14

el sol (el sol) sun 19, 26

la sombrilla (la som-**bree**-ya) beach umbrella 19

soñar (so-**nyar**) to dream 21

soplar (so-**plar**) to blow 8

el sube-y-baja (el soo-beh-ee-**ba**-ha) see-saw 7

el suéter (el **sweh**-tehr) sweater 10, 23

el supermercado (el soo-per-mer-**ka**-doh) grocery store 11

T

el tambor (el tam-**bor**) drum 6

la tarde (la **tar**-deh) afternoon 25

la tarjeta (la tar-**heh**-ta) card 22

la tarjeta de crédito (la tar-**heh**-ta deh **creh**-dee-toh) credit card 11

la taza (la **ta**-sa) cup 3

el techo (el **teh**-cho) roof 21

el teleferico (el teh-leh-**feh**-ree-ko) chair lift 23

el teléfono (el teh-**leh**-fo-no) phone 12

el tenedor (el teh-neh-**dor**) fork 3

el tiempo (el **tyem**-po) weather 26

el tigre (el **tee**-greh) tiger 14

las tijeras (las tee-**heh**-ras) scissors 5

la tiza (la **tee**-sa) chalk 5

la toalla (la toh-**a**-ya) towel 2, 19

el tomate (el toh-**ma**-teh) tomato 17

la torta (la **tor**-ta) cake 8

la tortuga (la tor-**too**-ga) turtle 14

la tostada (la tos-**ta**-da) toast 3

el trabajo (el tra-**ba**-ho) work 13

el trabajador de construcción (el tra-ba-ha-**dor** deh kon-strook-**syon**) construction worker 13

el tractor (el trak-**tor**) tractor 20

el traje de baño (el **tra**-heh deh **ba**-nyo) bathing suit 19

el transporte (el trans-**por**-teh) transportation 16

el trapo (el **tra**-po) cloth 12

el tren (el tren) train 16

tres (tres) three 29

el triángulo (el tree-**an**-goo-lo) triangle 6

el trineo (el tree-**neh**-o) sled 23

triste (**trees**-teh) sad 24

la trompa (la **trom**-pa) trunk (of an elephant) 14

la trompeta (la trom-**peh**-ta) trumpet 6

el túnel (el **too**-nel) tunnel 16

U

la uña (la **oo**-nya) fingernail 24

uno (**oo**-no) one 29

V

la vaca (la **ba**-ka) cow 20

el vaquero (el ba-**keh**-ro) cowboy 15

el vaso (el **ba**-so) glass 8

la vela (la **beh**-la) candle 8

el velero (el beh-**leh**-ro) sailboat 16

la ventana (la ben-**ta**-na) window 20

el verano (el beh-**ra**-no) Summer 28

el verde (el **ber**-deh) green 30

las verduras (las ber-**doo**-ras) vegetables 9

el vestido (el bes-**tee**-doh) dress 10

los vestidores (los bes-tee-**doh**-rehs) fitting room 10

vestirse (bes-**teer**-seh) to get dressed 1

el veterinario (el beh-teh-ree-**na**-ree-o) vet 14

la vía (la **bee**-a) track 16

el viento (el **byen**-toh) wind 26

el viernes (el **byer**-nehs) Friday 27

el violín (el byo-**leen**) violin 6

el violoncelo (el byo-lon-**seh**-lo) cello 6

volar (bo-**lar**) to fly 16

W

el windsurf (el **weend**-soorf) windsurfing 19

X

el xilófono (el see-**lo**-fon-o) xylophone 6

Y

el yogur (el yo-**goor**) yogurt 3

Z

el zafacón (el sa-fa-**kon**) garbage can 12

la zanahoria (la sa-na-**o**-rya) carrot 11

las zapatillas (las sa-pa-**tee**-yas) sneakers 1

el zapato (el sa-**pa**-toh) shoe 10

English-Spanish Glossary

A

afternoon la tarde 25
alarm clock el despertador 1
angel el ángel 22
ants las hormigas 18
apple la manzana 17
arm el brazo 2, 24
armoire el armario 1
Autumn el otoño 28
axe el hacha 17

B

backpack la mochila 5, 18
bag la bolsa 10
bakery la panadería 4
ball la pelota 1
balloon el globo 8
banana el platano 11
basket la canasta 9
bat el murciélago 21
bathing suit el traje de baño 19
bathroom el baño 2
bathtub la bañera 2
beach la playa 19
beach umbrella la sombrilla 19
bear el oso 14
bed la cama 1
bee la abeja 18
belt el cinturón 1
bench el banco 7
bicycle la bicicleta 7
big grande 10
bikini el biquini 19
bird el pájaro 17
birthday el cumpleaños 8
black el negro 30
blackboard el pizarrón 5
blanket la manta 1
blind man el ciego 4
to blow soplar 8
blue el azul 30
boat la barca 16
books los libros 5
boot la bota 18
bottle la botella 11
boy el niño 7
branch la rama 21
bread el pan 17
broom la escoba 12
brother el hermano 22
brown el café 30
bucket la cubeta 7, 19

bus el autobús 4, 16
bus stop la parada de autobús 4
butcher's la carnicería 9
butter la mantequilla 3
butterfly la mariposa 14
to buy comprar 9

C

cabin la cabaña 21
cake la torta 8
calendar el calendario 5
camcorder la cámara de vídeo 15
camera la cámara de fotos 8
campfire la fogata 21
can la lata 11
candle la vela 8
candy los dulces 8, 22
cap la gorra 18
car el coche 4, 16
card la tarjeta 22
carnival la feria 15
carpenter el carpintero 13
carrot la zanahoria 11
cash register la caja registradora 11
cashier la cajera 11
castle el castillo 1
cat el gato 2, 20
cauliflower la coliflor 17
cell phone el celular 4
cello el violoncelo 6
cereal los cereales 3
chair la silla 5
chair lift el teleferico 23
chalk la tiza 5
chaperone el chaperón 18
cheek la mejilla 24
cheese el queso 9
chicken el pollo 9
chicks los pollos 20
chimney la chimenea 21
chin la barbilla 24
chocolate el chocolate 8
chorus el coro 6
Christmas la Navidad 22
Christmas tree el árbol de Navidad 22
class la clase 5, 6
clock el reloj 12
cloth el trapo 12
clothes la ropa 10
cloud la nube 23
clown el payaso 15
coat el abrigo 10, 23

coat la chamarra 23
coat hook el colgador 5
cold el frío 23
colors los colores 30
to comb peinar 2
comb el peine 2
computer la computadora 1
conductor la directora 6
construction worker el trabajador de construcción 13
to cook cocinar 12
cook el cocinero 13
cookies las galletas 2
costumes los disfraces 15
country el campo 18
cow la vaca 20
cowboy el vaquero 15
crab el cangrejo 19
credit card la tarjeta de crédito 11
cub el cachorro 14
cup la taza 3
cupboard el armario 12
to cure curar 13
curtain la cortina 1
cymbals los platillos 6

D

to dance bailar 14
dancer la bailarina 13
darkness la oscuridad 21
daughter la hija 22
days los días 27
decorations las decoraciones 22
dentist la dentista 13
desk el escritorio 5
detergent el detergente 11
doctor el doctor 13
dog el perro 20
doll la muñeca 8
dolphin el delfín 14
door la puerta 3, 20
drawing el dibujo 5
to dream soñar 21
dress el vestido 10
to drive conducir 16
drum el tambor 6
duck el pato 20

E

ear la oreja 24
to eat comer 3

to eat breakfast desayunar 3
eggs los huevos 9
eight ocho 29
elbow el codo 24
elephant el elefante 14
entrance la entrada 11
eraser el borrador 5
eraser la goma 5
exit la salida 11
eye el ojo 24
eyebrow la ceja 24

F

face la cara 24
fairy el hada 15
farm la granja 20
farmer el granjero 20
father el padre 22
faucet el grifo 17
field el campo 20
finger el dedo 24
fingernail la uña 24
fire el fuego 22
fireman el bombero 13
fireplace la chimenea 22
firewood la leña 17, 21
fish el pescado 9
fish el pez 19
fitting room los vestidores 10
five cinco 29
flashlight la lámpara 21
florist el florista 4, 9
flower la flor 9, 18
flowerpot la maceta 35
flute la flauta 6
to fly volar 16
folder la carpeta 5
food la comida 12
foot el pie 2
forehead la frente 24
forest el bosque 18
fork el tenedor 3
fountain la fuente 7
four cuatro 29
fox el zorro 18
Friday el viernes 27
friends los amigos 7
frog la rana 21
frozen foods los congelados 11
fruit la fruta 9
fruit market el mercado de fruta 9

sausages las salchichas 9
scale la báscula 11
scarecrow el espantapájaros 17
scarf la bufanda 23
scissors las tijeras 5
scooter la moto 4
scooter el patinete 8
score la partitura 6
sea el mar 19
seal la foca 14
seasons las estaciones 28
see-saw el sube-y-baja 7
seven siete 29
sheep la oveja 20
sheet of paper la hoja 5
shell la concha 19
ship el barco 16
shirt la camisa 10
shoe el zapato 10
shopping las compras 9
shopping cart el carro 9, 11
shopping list la lista de compras 9
shoulder el hombro 24
shovel la pala 17, 19
shower la ducha 2
to sing cantar 6
singer la cantante 15
sink el fregadero 12
sink el lavabo 2
sister la hermana 22
six seis 29
skateboard el monopatín 7
skates los patines 7
to ski esquiar 23
skier el esquiador 23
skirt la falda 10
skis los esquís 23
sky el cielo 19
sled el trineo 23
to sleep dormir 1
slide la resbaladilla 7
slippers las pantuflas 1
small pequeño 10
snail el caracol 18
sneakers las zapatillas 1
to snow nevar 23
snow la nieve 23, 26

snowball la bola de nieve 23
snowman el hombre de nieve 23
soap el jabón 2
socket el enchufe 12
socks los calcetines 1
soda el refresco 8
son el hijo 22
to speak hablar 8
speedboat la lancha 16
sponge la esponja 2, 12
spoon la cuchara 3
Spring la primavera 28
squirrel la ardilla 18
star la estrella 21, 22
steps las escaleras 21
stereo el radiocasete 6
stocking el calcetín 22
stone la piedra 18
stove la estufa 12
strawberry la fresa 11
street la calle 4
streetlamp la lámpara 4
student la estudiante 13
to study estudiar 5
sugar el azúcar 3
Summer el verano 28
sun el sol 19, 26
Sunday el domingo 27
sunglasses los lentes de sol 19
swan el cisne 7
sweater el suéter 10, 23
to sweep barrer 13
to swim nadar 19
swing el columpio 7

T

table la mesa 12
tablecloth el mantel 8
tail la cola 14
to take llevar 11
to take a bath bañarse 2
tambourine la pandereta 6
teacher (m.) el maestro 5
teddy bear el oso de peluche 1
ten diez 29

three tres 29
thumb el pulgar 24
Thursday el jueves 27
tiger el tigre 14
tinsel la escarcha 22
to drink beber 7
to kiss besar 8
toast la tostada 3
toilet el inodoro 2
toilet paper el papel higiénico 2
tomato el tomate 17
toothbrush el cepillo de dientes 2
toothpaste la pasta de dientes 2
towel la toalla 2, 19
toys los juguetes 1
track la vía 16
tractor el tractor 20
traffic light el semáforo 4
traffic sign la señal de tráfico 4
train el tren 16
transportation el transporte 16
tray la bandeja 3
tree el árbol 21
triangle el triángulo 6
truck el camión 4
trumpet la trompeta 6
trunk (of an elephant) la trompa 14
t-shirt la camiseta 10
Tuesday el martes 27
tunnel el túnel 16
turtle la tortuga 14
two dos 29

U

underpants los calzoncillos 10

V

vegetables las verduras 9
vet el veterinario 14
violin el violín 6

W

waiter el mesero 13
to wash the dishes lavar los platos 12
washing machine la lavadora 12
wastepaper basket la papelera 5
water el agua 20
to water regar 17
water bottle la cantimplora 18
water skiing el esquí acuatico 16
watering can la regadera 17
watermelon la sandía 17
wave la ola 19
weather el tiempo 26
Wednesday el miércoles 27
week la semana 27
wheelchair la silla de ruedas 14
white el blanco 30
wind el viento 26
window la ventana 20
windsurfing el windsurf 19
Winter el invierno 28
winter hat la gorra 23
witch la bruja 15
wizard el mago 15
work el trabajo 13
to write escribir 5

X

xylophone el xilófono 6

Y

to yawn bostezar 21
yellow el amarillo 30
yogurt el yogur 3

Z

zoo el zoológico 14